EMPIRE HALTS HERE
VIEWING THE HEART
OF HADRIAN'S WALL

Detail from image B9 on page 67.

EMPIRE HALTS HERE

VIEWING THE HEART
OF HADRIAN'S WALL

Stan Beckensall

AMBERLEY

Detail from image B53 on page 98.

First published 2010

Amberley Publishing
Cirencester Road, Chalford,
Stroud, Gloucestershire, GL6 8PE

www.amberley-books.com

British Library Cataloguing in Publication Data.
A catalogue record for this book is available from the British Library.

ISBN 978 1 4456 0015 4

Typesetting and origination by Amberley Publishing
Printed in Great Britain

CONTENTS

Detail from image A56 on page 49.

ACKNOWLEDGEMENTS

I am grateful to Tony Iley and the *Hexham Courant* for the use of his aerial photograph on the cover, and to Matthew Hutchinson for his photograph of Portgate.

Lindsay Allason-Jones and Robin Birley, for whose work I have the highest regard, have contributed their personal choice of images to the book, and I am delighted.

I am very grateful to Kim Cowie for checking the text, and for making valuable suggestions. From Amberley Publishing, I would also like to thank Louis Archard for his editorial work and James Pople for the design of the book.

All the other photographs are my own, collected over twenty-five years, and are not artificially enhanced.

HADRIAN'S WALL

A place where empire halts.
Mist-haunted desolation holds in check
The will to move ahead.
And soldiers' eyes uneasily survey
Vast northern wastes;
An end to conquest, like a fire
That fades; but embers glow
And can be fanned into a flame.

A regiment of stone.
A geometric pattern coaxed from rock and soil,
Or forced persistently with toil.
Something to wonder at, admire;
Triumph of discipline
Ordering a landscape to obey.

Shut out the cold,
Stoke up the hypocaust,
Bring in our standards and our gods.

Each turret, fort and castle on the Wall
Becomes a reassurance of a different world.
The sound of marching, whiplash of command,
The clash of interlocking shields on alien soil;
Reaffirmation of the glory that is Rome.

Our hands rough-cut with mortar and sharp stone,
Legs stiff with pushing loaded carts through mud,
A finger broken on high scaffolding,
Thumb crushed by mauls in rock-cut ditch –
These were the lowest prices that we paid.
We joined the Legions, and we fought,
Became the masters of the north,
And our reward, as we are dwarfed,
Crushed in the shelter of our wall.
Housed in our barrack-blocks, patrolling roads,
Or dicing all our pay away
Is to be part of ranks on ranks of stone,
Cut to order, bound, by harsh winds flayed.

When I am dead
No one can really take my place.
This Wall will crumble, have to be rebuilt,
Fall down again, be quarried for its stone.
Yet I am part of it.
I lie in the foundations of a road,
Or feel the warm breath of calf in byre
Or watch a visitor admire the remnants of my work.

Stan Beckensall

PREFACE

The year 2009 marked the thirteenth pilgrimage to Hadrian's Wall, held at ten-year intervals since its beginning in 1849, when it was led by John Collingwood Bruce. Since 1930, the event has been accompanied by a handbook, which brings up to date the new discoveries and thinking about this frontier. The route is planned so that the 'pilgrims' can see for themselves major sites from Newcastle to Carlisle, although the defences do not end there; they go on to Maryport on the Cumbrian coast, and to a supply base at South Shields on the east. Interest in all aspects of the Wall grows each year.

I have been acquainted with this frontier since the late 1960s, although my specialisation in archaeology has been mainly in prehistory. I have lived close to it since 1977 (in Hexham), and have always found the landscape and history of the Wall fascinating. My acquaintance with Robin Birley and his family, dating to our shared role in teacher-training at Alnwick College of Education in the castle there, sparked my interest, and some of our trainees became directly involved in the excavations at Vindolanda. This site is actually south of the Wall, and was built on an earlier frontier known as the Stanegate, but it became a sizeable supply base and settlement, integral to the whole strategy of the Wall zone. Its archaeology has told us much about life on the frontier, and continues to do so every year. It has reminded us that troops sent to garrison England were not fighting all the time, and has taught us about how they, and civilians, lived there, placing more emphasis on domesticity than on warfare.

In the hundreds of years of its life, the Wall has changed, decayed, been attacked, abandoned, reoccupied; we can read some of these changes out in the field, and in the archaeological record. Even in its early stages, its planning changed, as we shall see. The reason for its being there at all is complex; in a sense, it was both a triumph and a failure. The Romans invaded Britain initially as part of a world-wide expansionist policy that targeted other nations for their wealth. Britain was at the edge of empire, but like all other parts of the Roman world it was brought to heel by force, and by offering the conquered the prospect of getting some advantage from Roman rule. It was a remarkable empire that incorporated so many different races, languages and traditions into an international state that demanded obedience and service in return. The physical realities of a good system of roads and well-managed settlements is what still remains, and innovations such as clean water supply, central heating for some, luxury goods, and strong government are well-known. These had their price, for the Roman army was an efficient and ruthless killing-machine, and the massacre of thousands of people was part of the process that the world paid for Roman rule by those who resisted it. This is the other side of the friendly 'Ermine Street Guard' displays.

The Roman army had conquered most of Britain by the time it moved to what is now Cumbria and Northumberland. The plan was probably to occupy and 'Romanise' the whole island, but this was abandoned after many attempts, and a frontier was drawn short of that mark. In this sense, the wall marks a failure to control completely the land north of it, but the Wall was not only a barrier but also a springboard for attack. The Stanegate frontier became an early frontier for further advance northwards, and was retained as the southern base for the construction of a new one, the site this time supposedly inspected by Hadrian himself, and certainly built to last, with the existing forts at Corbridge and Vindolanda being used as major back-up forts and settlements, both integral to the Wall strategy. A frontier further north into what is now Scotland, the Antonine Wall, was established, but shortly afterwards abandoned in favour of a return to Hadrian's Wall. There is nothing quite like it in the rest of the Roman world.

The building of the Wall was also prompted by the fact that there were thousands of troops in the North that needed to be kept busy and focused, so that when they were not fighting, they were building. One of the advantages of this army was that it was practised and efficient in construction work. In parts, the frontier was built of tuft and wood, with a bermed ditch providing some of the upcast for the Wall and the ditch counterscarp. At Birdoswald, to the west, is the only part where the stone and turf walls follow a completely different course for any length. Along both types of wall there were regularly spaced turrets and milecastles. Large forts, such as Coria and Vindolanda, and other auxiliary forts, formed a fighting base, but as the wall developed, the forts were moved to the Wall itself, and became part of it. Housesteads, for example, we know was built over an earlier turret (36b), and was thus an afterthought. Carrawburgh Fort was built over the Vallum.

There were many changes of plan, depending on political events and changing military needs. At first, the Wall was planned to be wider than it finished up in some places. The narrowing of the Wall needed less labour and materials, although many turrets and milecastles were built first with protruding stone wall wings that were meant to receive a similarly wide wall and didn't. In front of the Wall, unless it was a scarp slope, there was a ditch with a berm and counterscarp, but at Limestone Corner (not aptly named) the soldiers who were trying to dig through solid basalt gave up, leaving tool marks behind on some remaining unlifted blocks. We can visit the site and understand their frustration. The berm, it is now believed, could have had a line of pointed stakes or something similar, which would have the effect of modern barbed wire, to impede anyone who had managed to cross the ditch.

The Wall itself was massively tall, still surviving to three metres at its greatest height, yet in other places completely dug out. At Vindolanda, a replica wall has been built to give the sense of scale. When one thinks of this on top of the Whin Sill to the north, one can really sense the awesome achievement of the building. At the same site, a section of turf wall has also been built, with a wooden fence and tower. Both actions have made us see how much work was involved and how much material was required. The Wall connected the milecastles and turrets; two turrets equally spaced between milecastles, all with small garrisons, connections with each other by road, track, and signals. These could not withstand a big attack, but could get the message to the forts in time of trouble for the troops there to deal with the threat. A little more problematic is why they also built the Vallum – ditches and upcast mounds rather like a tramway running behind it, sometimes very close, and sometimes up to a kilometre away – especially as there is evidence that in places, parts were filled in to provide causeways across it soon after it had been dug. Generally, it was built later than the Wall. It has been seen largely as a barrier with checkpoints that defined the military zone – a very large 'Keep Out!'

To have built a wall of this size and length was a fantastic achievement, and is likely to have given a sense of pride to overseers and workers. There is no way that it could have been built by slave labour, but by legionaries and auxiliaries. It displays an intelligent use of geology and morphology in the areas that it crosses, and is particularly striking in the central section largely dealt with in this book. Here is the great Whin Sill outcrop, a series of basalt pillars in clusters that were once volcanic lava oozing along the fault lines in sandstones and limestones, cooling quickly so that the rock rapidly crystallised, and became very tough. Not only did this form a landscape that rises and falls suddenly, but it also produced rock that is now ideal for road surfaces, and was used in places to make a core for the Wall. It was very hard to quarry, even for experienced soldiery, but the skin of the Wall was best made from softer sedimentary rocks that, in the central section, are abundant. Quarries survive all along the course of the Wall, and stone was shaped into regular blocks on the outward face, and a pointed profile where the stones faced into the core. There was rubble, clay, and cement from limestone to bind it all together. The courses are regular, rising and falling with the land.

The nature of the Wall is determined by geology, so I shall devote much space to its landscape setting.

The pictures in this book explore all these features in the places where they best survive, showing also that the Wall became a convenient quarry for later generations, who found it easy to use ready-cut and shaped stone for their buildings. One particularly vicious attack on it was to use the base of the wall itself to make a road in the eighteenth century, when the English army needed to improve communications from Newcastle to the west to deal with Jacobite rebellions. Thus, for miles, motorists today drive over it, with the ditch to the north, and the Vallum to the south. There was also, relatively recently, a vogue for collecting Roman sculpture, and their altars are found in gardens, or used as fonts. The great monastery and cathedral of Wilfrid at Hexham has a seventh-century crypt built of stone from Coria, some of it from the Roman bridge there. Of particular value was decorated stone taken from the forts.

From its inception to its abandonment, the Wall and its buildings have changed, but it provided a focus for life at the edge of Empire. Its collapse is the collapse of Rome. Its survival is only partial, but much still lies beneath the surface, waiting to tell its tale. Past excavations have told us much, but more refined techniques are pouring out more and more information for us to interpret. Today, it is a World Heritage Site and attracts thousands of visitors each year, not just as part of the history of Rome but also as a place where the varied landscape at different times of the year is fascinating to those who enjoy journeying.

In choosing what to portray, I am aware that some parts are more exciting than others, and that most people find the central section the best. I share that, mainly because I can reach it so easily from my home, and frequently keep in touch with the excavations that are taking place. My images reflect that, but it is such an enormous subject that I cannot know or cover it all in sufficient detail to satisfy everyone. If it helps to develop in others a new way of seeing, and a desire to seek for more insights, I shall be happy. I shall be particularly happy if people begin to see life along the Wall as something that belongs not only to soldiery, but also to thousands of civilians. I also hope that we remember that the Wall zone is a living today for some farmers, and that we respect their rights to farm it.

Detail from image A16 on page 26.

COUNTRY THROUGH WHICH THE WALL PASSES

SOME GENERAL VIEWS

We shall follow the Wall from east to west in pictures, to see what kind of terrain the Romans used. Wherever possible, they made alignments from sighting point to sighting point in straight sections, allowing for deviations where there were obstacles, and for considerations of what would be visible from the top of the Wall.

KEY

—————— WALL
—————— VALLUM
◼ FORT

□ MILECASTLE
—————— TURF WALL
—————— STANEGATE
—————— RIVER
—————— ROAD

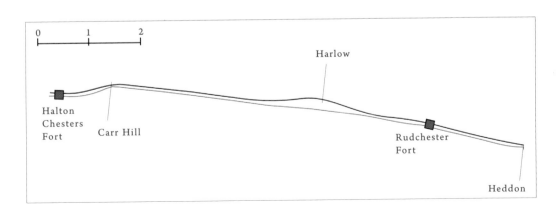

Beginning at **Heddon-on-the-Wall**, the short section of exposed wall has come through gently undulating ground, followed for most of its course by the Military Road, built in the 1740s.

From here, its course continues to the fort of **Rudchester**, which lies on higher ground, then continues this undulating course to **Harlow Hill**, heading toward **Halton Chesters** on a more or less straight course that, again, undulates gently. There is a kink in its path when it approaches high ground, above the fort of **Halton Chesters**, to keep land to the south more visible from the top of the Wall, for that is where all the major supplies would have been based.

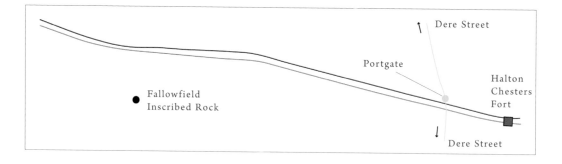

It reaches the **Portgate**, a gap in the Wall through which the main road of Dere Street from Corbridge runs north. From there, the land rises gently, but there is a steeper drop where it enters the North Tyne valley, and runs to the river-crossing by bridge at **Chesters**, a fort on the north bank. From here, a straight alignment takes the Wall to a hill at Walwick, from which the land dips, and rises again, to **Black Carts**, where the Wall lies to the north of the Military Road. Another hill gives an extensive view of the course towards **Carrawburgh Fort**, built next to a stream, from which its alignment continues directly to **Limestone Corner**.

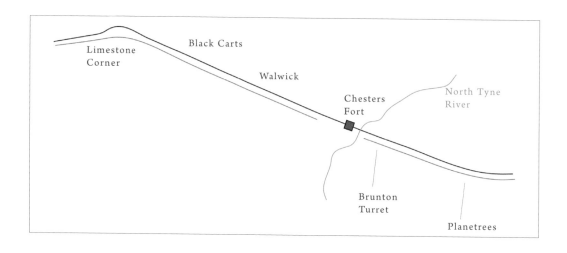

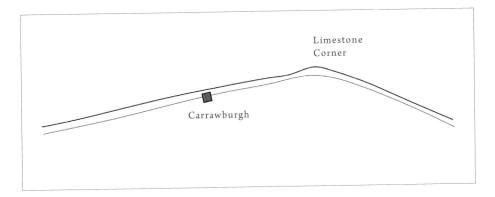

From here, the Military Road and Vallum bend to the SW, but the Wall and its ditch continue along **Sewingshields Crag**, before making a sharp turn south, from Turret 35a to Milecastle 36, then on to **Housesteads Fort**. We have now reached the spectacular change in Wall scenery, because the fault line in limestones and sandstones is shared by the intrusion of columns of basalt. From Limestone Corner, the basalt is cut into by Wall and Vallum, and from Sewingshields onward, the course of the Wall follows the crests, with the dip slope to the south, favoured by the Vallum and, further south, by the older Stanegate frontier. There are small loughs to the north of the scarp, and, after the drop to the north, the land gently rises to great swathes of marginally productive land, to what is now planted forest. The scarp edge is punctuated by 'nicks' – places where the basalt falls into small valleys – and the land on the south scarp has many channels running south. The Wall follows these natural features closely.

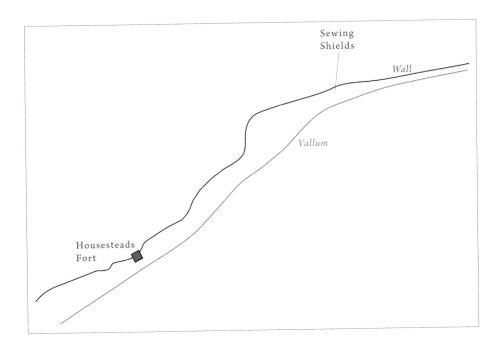

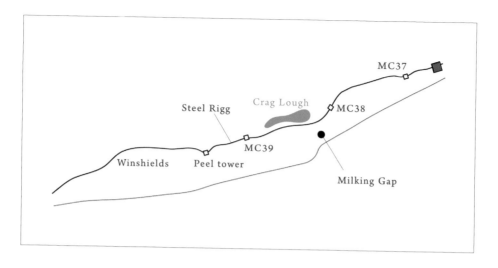

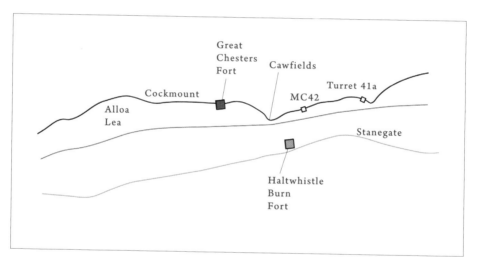

At **Cawfields**, the basalt ends abruptly where it has been quarried in recent times, and the wall is left high in the air. To the south, the Vallum runs along ground that has evened out, and in this area are many temporary auxiliary forts, visible in low lighting or snow, and the early Stanegate fort of **Haltwhistle Burn**. The Wall course then realigns slightly to head for the fort at **Great Chesters**, on more even land, with cemeteries, water mill, and quarries to the south, and an aqueduct coming in from the north-east.

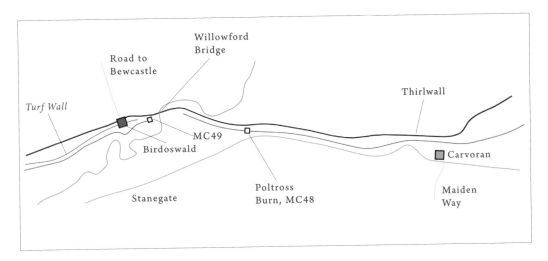

After Great Chesters, we encounter the whinstone again, often in clumps that rise above the grass, until a large chasm signals the beginning of Walltown Crags, dominating the country to north and south, to **Carvoran Fort** on the **Stanegate**. The Wall then heads for high ground above the River Irthing, which it crosses at **Willowford**. The north bank of the Irthing provides a small promontory high above it for a prehistoric enclosure, and a Roman fort at Birdoswald, where the ridge gives good views north and south, and a sighting point for another continuation of the Wall in a direct line to Pike Hill, where this pictorial survey stops.

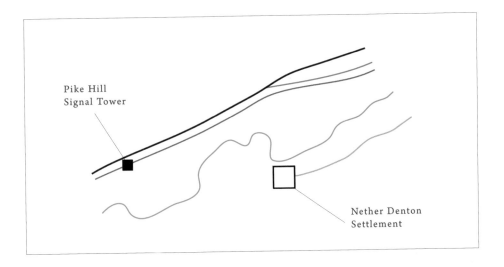

PART A: LANDSCAPES

1. Heddon-on-the Wall: The base of the 'broad' Wall runs east towards Throckley, with its filled and manicured ditch to the left, and the remains of the Vallum to the right. A medieval oven has been built into it.

2. Rudchester: The eighteenth-century Military Road cuts through the north of a severely denuded Roman fort towards Harlow. The fort was built astride the Wall.

3. Harlow Hill: The hill provided a good sighting point for surveyors. The Wall follows the undulating ground west.

4. Halton Chesters Fort lies below Carr Hill, beyond a single line of trees, the Wall here having been slightly diverted to the south from a straight course, from where it climbs the gentle slope to Portgate.

5. A view east from Carr Hill. The Military Road is built on the Wall base, with the Ditch to the left, and Vallum to the right.

6. Portgate is now marked by a roundabout, which directs the Roman Dere Street, now the A68, south to Corbridge, and north towards Scotland. The Wall runs left to right, east to west. (Matthew Hutchinson)

7. Planetrees, just as the Wall begins its descent to the North Tyne Valley. The Wall here has a broad base, but was built with a narrow one.

8. Brunton Turret (26b) was built above the river valley, en route for Chesters and Walwick. It has 'broad wall' wings to receive the Wall, but a change in plan narrowed the Wall.

9. Chesters Fort: We see the river (north to south), the bath house, fort, and underlying river terrace that has a large civilian settlement outside the fort walls. The Wall runs from the fort to the left (west).

Right:

10. Black Carts: The Military Road, parallel to the Wall, runs from Walwick at the bottom of the picture, with the Vallum to the left.

Below:

11. Black Carts: The Wall at ground level, looking from west to east.

12. Carrawburgh Fort, built astride the Vallum, and a later development in planning, has only a little to show. It lies east of a stream valley that houses a Mithraic temple and the site of Coventina's Well, in an area that was moorland.

13. Limestone Corner: The deep gash of an unfinished ditch, excavated out of basalt, gives wide views to the north, and from here begins to part company with the Military Road.

14. Limestone Corner: The Vallum proved equally difficult to quarry, but the path of its large ditch and flanking mounds to the south of the Wall is impressive.

15. Sewing Shields: The Wall has left the Vallum far to the south as it climbs the Whinstone Crags.

16. Sewing Shields: The breathtaking views to the north indicate why this line of crags was followed. Sandstone scarps outcrop at a lower level and small loughs, which were attractive to prehistoric people. Otherwise, there is an extensive spread of land, not suitable for arable farming, but acceptable for modern forestry.

17. Sewing Shields, west to Housesteads Fort.

18. Broomlee Lough, from the Wall which runs from Sewing Shields to Housesteads Fort.

19. Housesteads: to the north, it is built right up to the crag edge; this view from the south reveals the horizontal terraces crossed by rig and furrow systems of ploughing, that show its use as arable land from prehistoric times onwards.

20. Housesteads: the restored Wall crosses the Knag Burn from the east to become the fort's north wall.

21. West: the Wall continues its rolling course over the crags, with the Roman Military Way behind it.

22. The Wall descends to a stream valley, a farm, and the grass-covered remains of a milecastle.

23. The land drops steeply to Crag Lough, then takes a more gentle course to the north.

24. Crag Lough is one of the most attractive features of the Wall zone, where pillars of basalt rise vertically from the water.

25. From the west to Crag Lough.

26. Crag Lough, looking westward to Steel Rigg and Winshields.

27. Crag Lough westward: the Wall dips towards Sycamore Gap.

28. The steep descent to Sycamore Gap, where the Wall has been renovated recently.

29. The excavated Castle Nick Milecastle (39) marks another stage in the route westward.

30. The 'nicks' in the Whin Sill from the south, the tree marking Sycamore Gap. To the left, a milecastle occupies another 'nick'.

31. West of Castle Nick, from the east.

32. Steel Rigg: a sheer drop to the north and west.

33. Steel Rigg from the west in 1980, when people were once encouraged to walk along the level and grassed top of the Wall.

34. Steel Rigg from Winshields, looking east. The Wall Ditch is clearly defined in the snow, but the wall is a single-thickness rebuild.

35. Winshields Crag ascent, from the west.

36. Winshields Crag marks the highest point of the crags. Here, we look westward.

37. Winshields south: the northern edge is precipitous, but the southern face is broken by valleys.

38. The descent from Winshields to the Caw Burn, and the continuation of the Wall to the west.
    A turret base projects to the right from the Wall.

39. Towards Turret 40b base, where the Wall is paralleled by a modern field wall, creating
    another variation on the Wall zone geometry.

40. Milecastle 41 overlooks an extensive and exploited region, south of the crags to the Vallum and the Stanegate frontier, above the descent to the Caw Burn gap.

41. Caw Burn runs in a gap through the crags and gives us another extensive view of a land rich in remains of the past.

42. To the south is a large, relatively even tract of land, on which the Romans built many temporary camps. We see the Vallum and look south to the Stanegate frontier.

43. Towards Cawfields, the crag is more even on top, and gives particularly fine views south and west.

44. Milecastle 42, visible for miles around, is built on sloping ground. From here, the Wall climbs a crag which comes to an abrupt halt at a modern quarry.

45. Cawfields Quarry was only recently abandoned, and a noticeboard on site tells how it operated, sending whinstone to Haltwhistle. It is one of many abandoned industries along the Wall zone, including sandstone, coal, and limestone extraction.

46. The extraction left a huge hole, which is now filled with water, and lies beside a car park.

47. From here, the Wall and its deep Ditch run NW towards Great Chesters Fort in gently undulating country, in contrast to the crags.

48. Great Chesters lies on fairly level ground, has been roughly excavated in parts, has a farmhouse built into one corner, and to the west there are multiple ditches used for later rig and furrow ploughing.

49. Great Chesters Fort's west wall.

50. The Wall and Ditch run towards Cockmount Hill.

51. Cockmount, with a view to Steel Rigg and Winshields.

52. Alloa Lea, looking south to the Vallum.

53. Milecastle 44 and the recently-capped wall at Alloa Lea. The capping is to protect the underlying, collapsed original Wall, and to help the farmer control live-stock. It is an area of Special Scientific Interest for its plants and animals.

54. The Wall running westward from Alloa to Walltown Crags.

55. After another steep break in the basalt ridge, the Wall begins a steep climb up Walltown Crags.

56. Down the nick to Walltown Crags, the view dominated by a turret.

57. Walltown Wall and the whinstone outcrop, further west.

58. Walltown running north-west.

59. The view north from Walltown Crags – an extensive landscape of pasture and forest, leading to the Cheviot Hills.

60. End of the Wall, cut away by Walltown Quarry, later used as a rubbish dump, then levelled and planted.

61. Carvoran Fort is one of the Stanegate forts that has recently been shown from the air and geophysical survey to be an extensive settlement, despite there being little to see except grass. It lies south of the Vallum in this picture, to the right of the museum.

62. The Vallum at Carvoran, heading west for Gilsland.

63. Poltross Burn and the walkway over it to the milecastle.

64. The fenced Wall at Gilsland runs through a very untidy piece of land north of the Carlisle-Newcastle railway.

65. Willowford Bridge, across the River Irthing, towards Birdoswald Fort.

66. The Wall and Fort at Birdoswald lie above the River Irthing valley, seen here.

67. Birdoswald Fort south gate, facing the space occupied by a pre-Roman enclosure.

68. Turret 51b, on the stone wall west of Birdoswald.

69. Pike Hill Signal Tower is severed by the modern road.

70. Turret 52a marks the end of this pictorial survey of Hadrian's Wall where the turf Wall, replaced in stone, was built up to the stone turret. The view is east to Pike Hill and Birdoswald.

71. We are now back east, at Coria on the earlier frontier, the Stanegate, where it continued to supply the Wall zone and to hold a large garrison. Only a fraction of the fort is revealed, on a terrace above the River Tyne.

72. Coria lies to the south of the high ground where the Wall runs. The hillside was terraced for arable agriculture.

73. The Stanegate cannot be traced east of Coria, but to the west its distinctive route is overlaid by a modern road. Here it runs past Grindon Lough, with the Wall ridge to the right.

74. Barcombe Hill (or Thorngrafton Common) is a ridge of sedimentary rocks that commands views in many directions. Here it overlooks Vindolanda, and the continued course of the Stanegate uphill to the west.

75. The Wall ridge, seen from the same Barcombe viewpoint, with Housesteads to the left of the trees on the horizon, centre.

76. Haltwhistle Burn Fort is on the Stanegate, which comes in from the right (east) across an extensive stretch of land that includes many Roman temporary camps, the Vallum, quarries, and prehistoric standing stones.

77. The Stanegate's continued route westward is seen from Walltown Crags, blending in with sedimentary rock ridges and the Wall Vallum.

PART B: TOPICS

BEFORE THE ROMANS

We cannot assume that the Romans occupied an empty landscape, although their works must have eliminated many signs of previous occupation. In some places, 'ard marks', from the tips of primitive ploughs, have been found beneath the Wall, showing that some of the land was cultivated for arable crops. Many prehistoric sites are still visible, and there is evidence of activity going back to the hunter-gatherers of the Mesolithic (Middle Stone Age), through the agricultural changes of the Neolithic, to the ages of metal, in the form of implements, settlement, religious sites and burials.

Immediately prior to the Roman invasion, local people had for centuries been cultivating land and raising stock, as we see at sites like Warden Hill with its enclosures and terraces, living in scattered settlements, in round houses like the ones at Milking Gap – which was caught between the Wall and Vallum. These two sites serve as illustrations.

Warden enclosure is referred to popularly as a 'hillfort', and served as a local meeting place, perhaps for scattered farmers. There are many extra enclosures and field walls revealed from the air, some of which may be earlier or later than the fort. As the hilltop has a commanding view of the country around, and particularly of the course of the Stanegate early Roman frontier, there might have been a Roman signal station there. However, that has yet to be proved by excavation.

The little cluster of round houses reminds us of how different Roman landscape geometry was; people continued to live in these circular stone-based houses in the 'native' areas, and this adds to speculation about whether the Vindolanda 'rounds' catered for a similar local group (see illustration 74).

A link with a pre-Roman past is the adoption by the Roman army of local gods, to add to those already picked up over their world-wide conquered territories.

The excavation of Roman sites has been profitable in material goods and structures, and to people versed in the Classics, it was more interesting than what went before, or of a study of the local people, so much may have been overlooked.

1. Warden Hill prehistoric enclosure is on a hill which has many different phases of use, from Mesolithic to Medieval times. The earthwork itself is shown in this picture to have extensive added walls and hollows that are not yet satisfactorily interpreted. The village below is Fourstones.

2. The west entrance to the 'hillfort', with multiple ditches and walls, some denuded. The site may have been used by the Romans for a signal station.

3. Milking Gap marks a small, typical Iron Age settlement of enclosure wall and circular stone hut foundations, between Wall and Vallum.

THE WALL

What survives of the Wall varies considerably; its basic elements are, however, uniform. After a survey in straight sections, foundations were laid down and the wall was built, by three Legions, with shaped sandstone in tapered ashlar blocks that held in a rubble core, bound sometimes internally by clay or mortar, in regular courses held together by cement. The blocks are fairly uniform, and quite easily recognised if they have been re-used in other buildings. The courses generally follow the rise and fall of the land.

The Wall varied in thickness, and often shows a change in plan, from broad to narrow. Local stone was quarried nearby, and although it is difficult to 'date' a quarry, many along the line of the Wall must be Roman. One at Fallowfield has an inscription made by the man who quarried it. Some stone, especially for the core, would have come from digging the ditch in front of it.

The mortar used in the core, or to bind the courses, sometimes contained too much lime, which subsequently leaked down the wall, making it look to some as though it were the remains of limewash or rendering. Lime and coal are locally available.

The Wall is not a single period building, and has been rebuilt or repaired, so what we look at is not necessarily the original 'Hadrian's Wall'. There was a particularly big renovation, for example, in the reign of Severus. Even what we see now may be largely a Victorian rebuilding, and the flat top of walls is particularly suspicious on the Wall and in its buildings. In places, the line of the Wall is a thin, dry-stone rebuilding on the original foundation; in others, it has completely disappeared, especially where construction of the Military Road used its foundation and material for its own purposes, leaving the ditch itself to the north and the Vallum to the south to emphasise its course.

Modern conservation, following excavation, concentrates on solidifying what is actually left, in one part, by building a modern dry-stone wall on top of the tumbled original to protect it, and to enable the farmer to control the movements of his stock.

If we look carefully at field walls and buildings in the area, we can detect Roman stone that has been robbed and recycled in large quantities.

The highest surviving part of the wall is about three metres tall. Calculations have been made to work out what the Wall might have looked like when it was finished, and at Vindolanda, a replica has been built to make it easy to envisage. This has a walkway and a crenellated parapet, rises to a good height, and stands alongside a replica turf and timber wall. The Wall was not meant as a fighting platform for the whole of its length; the strategy was for it to act as a formidable barrier, fronted by ditch, berm, and counterscarp, from which signals could be sent to milecastles and forts to bring out a formidable army.

Visibility from the top of the Wall varies in its concentration north or south, but it has been suggested that the view to the south was particularly important to the surveyors, for most of the Roman troops were stationed behind it in Hadrian's day. Later, the forts were moved up to the Wall.

To the west, some of the Wall was originally built of turf and timber, and we see where, at Birdoswald, both walls are visible, because they take a slightly different route.

Above:

4. The regular stone courses of the Wall closely follow the rise and fall of the land. This section has been treated recently, leaving the core to protrude.

Right:

5. Ashlar: the Wall has regularly-shaped sandstone blocks that taper into the core, as we see here at Sewing Shields, forming an ashlar 'skin'.

6. The Wall core made use of any stone lying around and could include mortar or packed clay. It often survives when the ashlar has been robbed out for later building, as we see at Sycamore Gap.

7. Some original sections of the Wall survive in fallen parts, as we see at Alloa.

Above:

8. There is an example of a changed alignment of the Wall to the east of Milecastle 39, revealed by excavation, with the later insertion of a shieling – a shelter for herdsmen – at the top.

Right:

9. At Sewing Shields, we have one example of two widths of Wall; the early plan was a broad-based wall, and later this was narrowed.

Overleaf, page 68:

10. Brunton Turret was built with wings to receive a wide wall, but this was narrowed.

11. As the Wall was robbed of its top courses, or even the whole structure in places, it is rare to have a section of this height, seen at Walltown.

12. If mortar contains too much lime, there might be a white seepage. This has given rise to the idea that the wall was 'whitewashed', but there is no real evidence for this.

Left:

13. A recent consolidation at Sycamore Gap shows the foundations of the Wall, regular ashlar courses and rubble core.

Below:

14. At Alloa Lea, a tumbled stretch of Wall has been preserved by capping it. This also enables the farmer to control stock. Stone used is newly-quarried, announcing that it is modern.

15. The extent of the robbed-out Wall can be seen on the east Walltown Crags, reduced to a low mound that follows the cliff edge.

16. The Romans rebuilt their walls, and so did later farmers who wanted them as field walls. At Great Chesters, we see this large Roman decorative slab reused.

COMPONENTS

The Wall, as we have seen, was accompanied by a ditch, berm, and counterscarp. Whether the general inclusion of stakes or other deterrents on the berm applied to much of the Wall has yet to be proved.

The **Ditch** has survived well because it escaped robbing. It has gradually silted up, and was once much deeper and steeper-sided than it appears today. The frustration of digging it is no better seen than at Limestone Corner, where huge blocks of Whinstone had to be quarried, and the ditch was left unfinished. Yet it was only in exceptional places, such as the edge of cliffs, where the Wall came close to the edge, that the ditch was omitted.

Some material from the ditch provided the material for the counterscarp, and for the core of the Wall.

The width of the Wall was planned as a broad one (3 m thick); the wings of milecastles and turrets that were built first to receive it were built on the assumption that it was to be broad. When the Wall was narrowed (to 1.8 m), an adjustment was made, so that they have wings wider than necessary.

Milecastles, small forts built at every Roman mile, were intended for provisioned garrisons of troops with horses that could sally forth to meet trouble, so there were gates to the north and south. As strategy changed with the building of forts, these gateways were modified, especially with the blocking of the north gate, and their narrowing. They were linked by the Military Way on the south. Inside the milecastles were one or two barrack blocks, stabling and a cooking area.

Two **turrets** were built between milecastles, for a small number of men, with no gate to the north, but some of these were soon demolished when they became redundant.

The **Vallum** has survived well in places as an impressive monument. Its purpose is not crystal-clear, but it was established as a security barrier, rather than as a defence to the south of the Wall; official crossing places that could direct traffic through the milecastles controlled traffic movement. Civilians could drive stock along the north berm of the Vallum, and be directed through 'official' crossing places. Elsewhere, it directed people to the forts. A massive, linear, flat-bottomed ditch, flanked by mounds excavated from it, it follows the Wall at varying distances according to terrain and, at times, swerves away, up to a kilometre away. As the forts came later than the Wall, the Vallum, contemporary with them, was affected by the change in strategy.

Many causeways were later created over the ditch so that traffic was less obstructed. Like the ditch to the north of the Wall, it became silted up. Parts were later filled in and the area ploughed, but it is still faintly visible even there.

17. We see the ghost of the Wall and ditch, the berm, and counterscarp below Walltown Crags from the east.

18. The ditch west of Sewing Shields, where it was dug even where the Wall ran very close to the crag edge, although some of the crag could have fallen away since then.

19. Great Chesters: agriculture has destroyed much, but the Wall Ditch is still very pronounced.

20. Milecastles have suffered the same fate as other buildings, but there are good examples of their structure and changes. Castle Nick shows the excavated layout of the interior in snow.

21. A milecastle at Crag Lough has walls reduced to grass mounds.

22. Poltross Burn Milecastle (M48) was one of the first to be excavated properly, in 1909, and supplied important dating evidence. It lies on a steep slope, a drop of about 3 metres.

23. Poltross Burn Milecastle north, where stone steps lead to the upper level and Wall, giving some idea that its height was 4.3m.

24. The barracks inside are built on a steep slope. Awkward, perhaps?

25. Sewing Shields Milecastle revealed on excavation that it had been reused in Medieval times for building a shieling. The name 'shields' appears frequently, as it means a temporary building or buildings where herdsmen could watch over their animals away from the main settlement in summer.

26. Housesteads Milecastle (M30) has many important features, such as a blocked north
    gateway, and very high surviving walls with masonry courses, including a thin layer of
    stones. It has a rare survival of an arch over its north gate, too.

27. Cawfields is probably one of best-known of all milecastles, not only for its position on a
    slope, but also for the survival of its gateways – the northern one being redundant from the
    outset (see illustration 44).

28. There were two turrets between milecastles. Brunton Turret is a particularly good survival, with its threshold step and much of its lower stonework intact (see illustration 8).

29. Walltown Turret is dramatically situated, and has the remains of its entrance arch inside on the ground (see illustration 56).

30. The Vallum at Carvoran survives mainly as a ditch. Where excavations have taken place, the Vallum usually has a flat base.

31. At Limestone Corner, the builders had the same problem of cutting through solid basalt as they did with the Wall Ditch. Here the Vallum is a ditch flanked by two mounds, with an extra low mound to the south (see illustration 14).

32. The same Vallum from the west, where it has been built over in many places, forming causeways.

33. One of the finest stretches of Vallum is seen here at Cawfields, where crossings over it are also clear.

34. The Vallum at Cawfields seen from the air.

BRIDGES

The Romans would have used many fording places across streams and rivers, probably already used by local people, but as the Wall strategy developed, it became necessary to build bridges to carry the Wall and traffic across these obstacles. They already had considerable experience of this type of building. In this area there are three particularly fine examples from east to west: Coria, Chesters and Willowford.

At **Coria**, recent flooding and erosion led to a decision to excavate the south bank where the bridge began its span to the major settlement on the other side. A heap of massive, shaped stones is the result, saved from further damage, and with their original positions carefully recorded. They have distinctive Roman tooling, often seen in buildings that have re-used them, some of which are clear in the crypt of Hexham Abbey, used there in the seventh century. Sufficient information has been accumulated to reconstruct what the finished bridge might have looked like.

At **Chesters,** further west along the Tyne, remains of the abutments have been found on both sides of the river, the more interesting being on the east side, where the Wall runs up to it from Brunton Turret. The excavation of the west bank is more recent, and there is little to see now, but the report carries the details. Like that at Coria, it was carried over the river on strong piers, rebuilt in the third century. As the River Tyne has flooded many times in recent history, it is safe to assume that it would have done so before, and that repairs and modifications had to be made. A ramp carried the road up to the bridge, and this crossed it. The bridge was well-decorated, as we see from some of the carved stone left behind, mostly from the third century re-building.

Willowford Bridge in Cumbria was also rebuilt, and evidence points to the earliest Hadrianic bridge being made of stone rather than timber; it would have carried the Wall over the river. Some signs of this remain, but flooding caused it to be rebuilt in wood before a new one was built of stone in the early third century. That building eased the pressure of water on it, and allowed the bridge to be wide enough to carry a road over – as it did at Chesters.

The later narrow wall that was built over it sits on the bottom five courses of the broad wall.

35. A recent excavation of the rampart approach to Coria, on the south bank of the Tyne, rescued these massive, shaped blocks, now displayed above flood level.

36. Chesters Bridge east: a fine piece of engineering, the latest bridge being third-century. This picture, and the two that follow, show where the Wall reaches a tower, and is carried over the river from a well-constructed abutment.

37. Chesters Bridge abutment.

38. Chesters Bridge foundation east, designed to carry a road across. An earth ramp carried the road to the stone tower. Later, a water channel was built through the base of the tower to serve a mill downstream.

39. Chesters Bridge west: a recent excavation has uncovered the structure, but it has now been buried.

40. The Willowford Bridge spanned the River Irthing, the course of which has shifted. First made of wood, it was replaced by stone in the mid-second century.

41. Willowford Bridge tower and overflow channel.

FORTS

Some of the forts are the most impressive survivals on the frontier; some are more thoroughly excavated than others and well-displayed for visitors, but the rest are hard to pick out in the landscape casually. They have a 'playing card' plan, shared with their temporary camps, and their provision changed the building timetable, so that some buildings on the Wall had to be demolished, and ditches filled in to accommodate them. Wherever possible, they had to project north, and this emphasises that they were meant to pour out an army to meet a threat, and not just to protect its garrison, although the latest at Carrawburgh and Great Chesters did not project beyond the Wall, as it was not necessary. They had to hold infantry, some exclusively at Housesteads, Birdoswald and Great Chesters; others had cavalry, such as Chesters fort, and some were mixed. There were already forts to the south of the Wall, so these were additions, not replacements. Concentration on their building took away resources from the rest of the Wall, so that one result was that the latter was built narrower to save labour, time and materials. At Birdoswald, the Wall was realigned to make more space available behind it for the fort.

The pictures show where these forts were sited; their structures were very similar, but changes in terrain were taken into consideration, and were affected by the period when they were built. The most spectacular siting is **Housesteads** on the Whin Sill. Here, the crags provide a breath-taking height from which vast, open country is overlooked. Not far to the south-west lies **Vindolanda**, already built long before, lying in a sheltered area with the land rising around it. These two, with their contrasts, are perhaps the best to visit, especially as they have been well excavated in the past and present. As a contrast to these, there is not much to see at **Carrawburgh**, although it is not without interest; the site lies on what must have been wild moorland beside a stream, and the fort was built over the Vallum – so it was an addition. To the far west, **Birdoswald** shares, like Housesteads, a site with extensive views, especially to the south, where it overlooks the valley of the River Irthing. It also shares a programme of recent excavation that is on-going, and has been carefully prepared for visitors.

To the east, **Rudchester** is hardly noticeable from the Military Road which cuts through it, and much of it has rig and furrow ploughing, which shows that it has been intensively farmed. Excavation has not led to reinstatement; a large coloured notice-board reconstructs what it might have looked like, but walkers must find it difficult to reconcile this with what can actually be seen. Further west, **Halton Chesters**, where there is little to see, is also cut by the Military Road, lying in a dip close to the Portgate: the Wall alignment dips south towards it, rather than running straight on, suggesting that the view to the south was more important than the north, for that is where **Corbridge** is, a major settlement that has been extensively excavated, has much left to be dug, and is well displayed on site, and with a museum. Like Vindolanda, this was built on the earlier Stanegate frontier.

Chesters lies in more open country, suitable for cavalry, with a bridge crossing. It has been excavated and its structures have been rebuilt, manicured, and displayed, and it has an impressive museum.

On the Stanegate, **Carvoran** is the only fort for which we have an accurate date, being rebuilt in stone in AD 136-7. There is little to see for this, but there is a modern museum concentrating on the Roman Army linked closely with Vindolanda, and a splendid picture of the geophysical survey that has revealed a dense and wide spread of buried buildings in and around the fort.

Great Chesters has been dug into; there are some features such as gateways, and a strong room, but the site is notable for its position, especially the views to the south and east. A farm occupies the north-east corner.

All of these forts have similar buildings in their interiors, and the pictures are chosen to illustrate some of these features, for they were garrisons, with accommodation for troops and horses, equipment, food stores, workshops, ovens, latrines, a central headquarters, strong room, chapel of the standards, commanding officer's house, hospitals, and baths. They might not have the mosaics and other luxuries seen in other parts of Roman Britain, but they did have a degree of comfort that contrasted with what the locals experienced, although the 'vici' built outside the forts in stone must have given at least some of the local population a share in some of the benefits of Roman rule.

42. Rudchester Fort: there is little to be seen, although the results of excavations are displayed on a panel that shows what the whole fort might have looked like. It extended north beyond the Wall on a relatively flat area.

43. Halton Chesters: on a site of low land that slopes gently to the south, the Fort protrudes north of the Wall. The grassed interior has traces of buildings and has been ploughed. The Vallum running through is a strong feature.

44. The site chosen is a river terrace, although it is overlooked by hilly country to the north. The excavated part is only a fraction of what lies here. The Stanegate runs through the centre of the settlement, and Dere Street to the east runs north to south.

45. Chesters Fort has a clear layout, with headquarters, commander's house, and barracks at the centre, and gates and turrets clearly revealed. Around the fort are other buildings under grass, with strong signs of rig and furrow ploughing that would have cut into these. The area would have been ideal for cavalry.

46. Carrawburgh: although there is little to see inside the Fort, many come to see the Temple of Mithras, excavated in the stream bed close to the site of Coventina's Well (see illustration 12).

47. Housesteads Fort is not only dramatically situated on the crag edge, but also it is one of the most extensively excavated and displayed of all the forts. Its civilian settlements, field systems that include terraces and rig and furrow and external religious sites, make the picture even fuller (see illustration 19).

48. This picture, taken in 2010 from the hill overlooking Vindolanda from the east, includes recent excavations and the course of the Stanegate uphill from the Fort.

49. Birdoswald Fort occupies a promontory, with the River Irthing below, used by pre-Roman people, and an extensive stretch of land that became settled outside the fort too, seen here to the east, its buildings buried.

50. The 'Granary', where all kinds of foodstuffs were stored, has a well-preserved base at Coria. The buttresses show that it was a tall, strong building.

51. The Coria Granary, seen from the south, shows where the carts would have unloaded on to a platform just off the Stanegate.

52. Granaries at Vindolanda are a recent discovery, and they are now being consolidated. (2010)

53. At Housesteads, the granaries were at first a two-storeyed, buttressed building, with a roof supported by pillars. The building was then divided by walls. Small pillars supported the floor, under which air could circulate. Grindon Lough is in the background.

54. The buttressed granaries at Birdoswald, recently excavated, were found to have been used for the flooring of a 'Dark Age' building after the Roman army had been recalled from Britain.

55. At Vindolanda there are two latrines, this one to the south, capable of seating many people on seats that were above the parallel drains.

56. The Housesteads latrine is justifiably one of the most famous buildings in the fort.

57. This emphasises the care that went into good hygiene, and the ingenuity of the Roman engineers who used water from roof tops and other sources, stored in tanks, to flush effluent onto the fields outside.

58. At Coria, we see the aqueduct that supplied water to the fountain by the main road.

59. The fountain at Coria, with its crafted stone slabs and lead-filled joints, seen from the south-west.

60. The Coria fountain lies to the left of the road and alongside the granaries. Top left is a large, unfinished courtyard building.

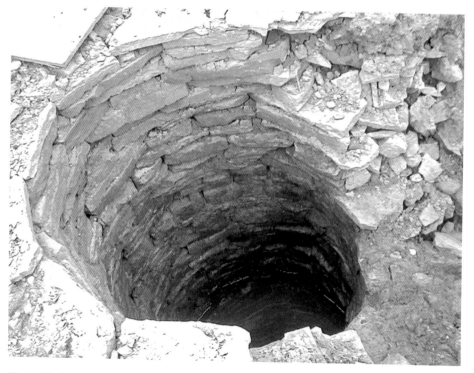

61. At Vindolanda there are many wells, drains, and channels to be seen to the west. This well has been excavated and covered over; when it was discovered, it had Roman altars dumped in it between one phase of fort-building and another.

62. Close to a river, with other water being piped into the Fort, Chesters still had use for a well within the headquarters building.

63. At Birdoswald Fort there are many ovens close to, or built into, the fort walls.

64. At Chesters Fort, this oven is situated within the west gate tower.

65. Of great importance to the fort garrisons were bath houses, not only for cleanliness, but also a place where people could socialise. The one at Chesters is an outstanding example that has been used as the basis of a replica at Wallsend Fort. It lies just above the north bank of the river.

66. A view from the south, showing how well, and by how much, the walls have survived.

67. The apses are thought to be either for statues, or were used as cupboards for changing.

68. The early bath at Vindolanda lies in the south-east sector.

69. The bath house lies outside the latest fort, and is a fine survival.

70. Although the Wall forts do not have mosaic floors, some of the principal rooms have underfloor hypocaust heating, as we see at Chesters and at the two forts pictured next.

71. A hypocaust system at Vindolanda.

72. The hypocaust in the commander's large courtyard house at Housesteads.

73. Vindolanda hypocaust at the centre of the headquarters complex.

74. Vindolanda's fort walls were often repaired or rebuilt, as we see in this section, which is uniquely built over round-house foundations.

75. The 'playing card' shape of fort walls is seen in the rounded corner at Housesteads, south-west.

76. Early excavators at Chesters concentrated on reinstating features that did not include a continuous fort wall.

77. Recent excavations at Birdoswald were responsible for exposing this 'monumental' part of the west wall that is so different in the way the stone is shaped and held together that it might have had a monument built on top of it.

78. The east wall at Birdoswald has interesting layers of stone, especially the use of a thin band.

79. Fort gateways gave an important prestigious message to those who approached them. Here is a particularly fine example at Housesteads, west, with double entrances.

80. Very often fort gateways were partly blocked to narrow the flow of traffic. At Great Chesters, the west gate is inserted into a wall which has many buildings attached to it.

81. The denuded south gate at Great Chesters has a displaced altar close to its entrance.

82. The north gateway at Vindolanda has many signs of change, with earlier masonry outside and inside (see illustration 74).

83. The east gate at Birdoswald is one of the finest survivals, and has part of its arch intact.

84. Detail of the arch at Birdoswald.

85. Barrack blocks were another essential provision in forts. At Housesteads, excavation has shown a change in plan, from long rectangles split into regular rooms to a more spacious 'chalet' type of building.

86. Chesters Fort has some of the most complete barrack block foundations, although the regularity of the wall tops suggests some rebuilding and tidying up in the late nineteenth and early twentieth centuries, as we see also on the Wall.

87. Two army units had their own compounds side by side at Coria, to the south of the Stanegate.

88. The headquarters was the nerve centre of the fort. We see this in the latest fort built at Vindolanda.

89. Chesters has a large open space flanked by buildings, used for assembly and parades.

90. Housesteads has pillars that would have formed an impressive feature in the headquarters building.

91. The strong room, where money and, perhaps, the sacred standards were kept, was of enormous importance and, as we see at Great Chesters, was built underground, though little is left of it.

92. Chesters has a fine example of a strong room, part of the headquarters complex.

93. At Coria, one military compound had its own strong room, well-preserved

94. The commander had his own elaborate suite of rooms, usually round a courtyard, both as a reminder of Rome and of his status. At Chesters, the eastern part has its own bath house.

95. The fine courtyard building for the commander was built on a platform of levelled
whinstone because of the slope at Housesteads. Some of the rooms were well-heated.

96. At Housesteads, the vicus was made up of buildings outside the fort walls, all round it, and here we see the Roman-type building in stone, south, probably built by the army.

97. Although all the forts are known to have extensive extra-mural settlements, those at Vindolanda are the most thoroughly explored. Part of the vicus lies on the foundations of the Severan fort, to the west of the final fort building.

ROADS

The earliest Roman road is the **Stanegate**, a frontier rather than a defence, which linked together forts to the south of Hadrian's Wall, some of which continued to act as crucial supply-bases. The word means a stone road; in places it is now tarmaced, wide, and runs in straight sections. The eastern parts are not traced, but the western section is clear. The forts and fortlets linked were at Corbridge, Newborough, Vindolanda, and Haltwhistle Burn, then further west to Carvoran, south of Poltross Burn, south of the River Irthing to Denton, just outside the area covered in this survey.

The Wall may have been a line of demarcation between the Romans and the *Brittunculi*, but it was not a static frontier; roads ran from south to north to outlying forts. **Dere Street** crosses the river at Coria, and has a gateway to the north at Portgate, where the A68 follows its course generally. The road is like a switchback, but in straight sections that ride over undulating natural ridges. It is a very important survival of Roman engineering.

At Carvoran, the Roman 'Maiden's Way' runs in from the Alston area to meet the Stanegate.

Further west at Birdoswald, another important road runs north to Bewcastle (Fanum Cocidi), where there is a large fort taken over by a Norman castle in one corner, close to one of the most famous Saxon crosses.

To the south of the Wall, running close, is the **Roman Military Way**, provided later, which links the defences. In places it is bolstered by a strong kerb, cobbled beneath the grass and part of its clearest route is now used as a footpath.

Right:

98. The Stanegate main road runs to the north of Vindolanda, but inside the main military and civilian buildings, a well-paved road survives.

Below:

99. At Coria, the Stanegate runs east to west through the Fort, and Dere Street runs north to south a little to the east.

100. A large part of the Stanegate, like this from Vindolanda to Newborough with Grindon Lough to the left, is used today.

101. Dere Street leaves the Wall zone at Portgate, heading north in a series of straight alignments that rise and fall dramatically over natural ridges.

102. The Military Way was a road running behind the Wall, following its course closely. Here we can follow it as a green path west of Housesteads

103. At Crag Lough, the wide Military Way has been badly used by a heavy tractor. (2010)

EXCAVATIONS

The Wall has been the target of digging for centuries, as a quarry for dressed stone, a source of curiosity and treasure and for scientific exploration. With new techniques available, Roman archaeology is more precise than ever, and concentrates not only on structures, but also on the minutiae of life revealed by sealed soil deposits, especially of organic matter, particularly at sites like Vindolanda, where ongoing excavations constantly reveal things that can change our thinking. Other sites like Housesteads, Corbridge, and Birdoswald have played a major role in this too, and have opened up more for the public to see. Some excavations have set out to answer specific research questions, and we have a considerable archive of reports from many generations that take our understanding further, without having answered all the questions that we ask. Sometimes, there are surprises like the discovery of the 'extra' tower at Peel Gap.

As the Wall has become more accessible, there is a need to excavate, reinstate, and safeguard, and this provides further opportunities for archaeology.

From excavations of all periods there have been changes in the way we think about it, especially in the focus on life on the Wall for civilians, as well as for the military. The Vindolanda writing tablets have particularly added life to archaeological discovery. We can see people with names and lives, not just those on tombstones or memorials, we have more insights into how they lived, and the value of the tablets has been recognised as an important national treasure. The special conditions of preservation on the site, through the habit of the army of levelling a fort before building another on top, and the unique conditions that have saved it all for us have revolutionised the study. There is still so much to be found there.

Because it is such a costly process, and has to be weighed against other uses we make of money, each excavation must have a well-defined purpose. New and important discoveries lead to more tourist sites, and some of the income from this has to be reinvested in archaeology.

I have chosen modern excavations for my picture focus, as I have observed them and taken part at one site.

104. The depth of deposits from different period forts has made excavation difficult, but
     rewarding. This area west of the latest fort has a vicus building nearest the camera built
     over considerably early deposits.

105. In the same area, a buried road is flanked by a ditch terminal on the right. Black layers
     preserved considerable organic material.

106. Further west, outside the forts, is a complex area that includes workshops and shrines, the top heavily ploughed out. Most has now been re-covered.

107. A road surface between buildings and the west fort wall is being meticulously excavated in late 2009. A large 'patch' of coins was found.

108. In 2009, the north-west quadrant of the latest fort was excavated, revealing barrack blocks and a unique shrine built within the north fort wall.

109. The final stage in excavations and reinstatement at Housesteads Fort on the barrack blocks, looking east.

110. Recent excavation revealed a uniquely placed additional turret/tower at Peel Gap, with a bank of stone against it, thought to be a ramp or stairway.

111. The same site later.

112. An excavation at Castle Nick (M39) revealed that only half had traces of the earliest phase of building. It continued in use with only a small number of men, but exactly how many is not known.

113. Castle Nick had a hard road surface between internal buildings.

114. The excavation of Chesters west bridge abutment added to what was known from the east, with a considerable amount of stonework, but the site has been re-covered.

115. The excavation of Chesters west end of the bridge.

116. Excavations at Birdoswald continue, and have recently included a Time Team presence. Under Tony Willmott's direction, one of the most interesting discoveries was the excavation of a hall built over the Granaries after the Roman army had left Britain (see illustration 54) and this stretch of monumental masonry at the west gate (with Tony).

117. Also uncovered and displayed at Birdoswald is another part of its later history, when it was used by Border reivers for a tower.

FINDS

Digging up the past has often been motivated by greed at one extreme, and a genuine desire to learn on the other.

A particularly fine piece of jewellery or sculpture hits the headlines. Out of context, these things may be of limited value to the archaeologist; a sealed-in layer of soil may be much more important, but that is not so exciting for the public generally. The chance of survival of domestic ware, such as leather and clothing, is minimal, unless it is deeply buried in conditions that have arrested its decay. Stone objects, chipped and broken though they may be, have a greater chance of survival. Statues, for example, may be of a variety of gods that have come from all parts of the 'Roman' world. People die or wish their achievements to be known, inscribed in stone. Legions record their presence. Altars, temples, and images survive. Discoveries may be lying on the ground, in hedges, used as building material, appear in people's gardens, and are occasionally unearthed by accident. Roman wells, because water from time immemorial has been sacred, may become the repository of offerings, or even a place where altars are dumped when the troops move on. Many of these objects are now stored in museums, where they add considerably to the record of what has happened, along with pottery, tools, ornaments, clothing, millstones, and even a wig.

The pictures that follow, and those provided at the end by Lindsay Allason-Jones and Robin Birley, give examples of just of few of these saved objects, out of hundreds.

118. At Vindolanda there is a constant stream of finds that add to the story of people living there. Here is one example of a brooch in the palm of an excavator, when it was trowelled from the black mud.

119. The Wall zone has given up a considerable number of statues and inscriptions, like this in honour of the goddess Coventina from Carrawburgh, where her well was sacred.

120. At the same location, the Temple of Mithras, a Persian god originally, is now well displayed, although the altars seen here are replicas. The originals are in the Great Museum of the North, where much floor space is given to Rome.

121. At Vindolanda, there is a display of replica Roman tombstones which give vital information about who was stationed where, and what gods they served.

122. At Vindolanda, the technology of Roman building and manufacturing is remarkably preserved and displayed. Here are some tools that could still be in use today.

123. Archaeology today has different priorities from those of early excavators. At Vindolanda, the survival of all kinds of animal bones shows not only what people ate and used, but also what kind of small or microscopic life existed then.

RECYCLING

The amount of dressed stone along the Wall has always been a tempting quarry for builders, and a cursory examination of buildings and field walls close to it reveals a considerable amount of re-used stone. The Anglian churches along the Tyne have such stone incorporated, especially in the quoins of their towers; Corbridge church has an arch taken from the headquarters building at Coria, Chollerford church may have used Roman pillars, and the seventh-century monastic church of St Wilfrid has a crypt that is built of Roman stone, probably from Coria. Much of Halton is built of Roman stone from the fort there, and the graveyard has a Roman altar.

124. Recycling is part of history, as we see in this garden wall at Corbridge, where part of a Roman quernstone imported from Germany has been built into it.

125. Halton churchyard has a Roman altar, put there in Victorian times. Many of the stones in the tower and other buildings there are from the fort.

126. At Chollerton church it is possible that these pillars came from Chesters Roman Fort.

127. Hexham's original seventh-century church and monastery made use of Roman stone both from the fort and bridge at Coria.

128. The Monument to Flavinus, a young cavalry officer stationed at Coria, lay in the foundations of a wall in the same building.

Above:

129. Thirlwall 'Castle', the name meaning a gap in the Wall, took stone from the Wall to build it.

Right:

130. At Warden, this Roman tombstone was split and reused for an Anglian grave, now in the church porch.

PUBLIC ACCESS
AND PRESENTATION

Centuries ago, the Wall zone was a dangerous place, a deterrent to travellers and antiquarians. Today, it has 'open access' through specially-negotiated footpaths. It has become a business, with millions of pounds coming to the area from tourism. This generates problems, though, for the hill-farmers through whose land it passes, and for conservationists. On the other hand, it is a superb area of British countryside, full of interest, which should be open to all.

In 2010, the Wall had a series of beacons lit at intervals from east to west, at a cost of some £300,000, which claimed to have brought in an extra £1 million in tourism. It may have been spectacular for those with tickets who were close enough to see it, but it became a problem for farmers and other local people, and for many who found themselves nose-to-tail in a convoy of cars along the Military Road. It provided TV and the press with a spectacle, however. This illustrates one problem of the Wall's success.

The Hadrian's Wall footpath means that people can now follow a secure route that is particularly valuable in this section of the Wall. Stiles have been built, field walls reinforced, some paths strengthened, and more facilities made available, although erosion of the most used tracts remains a problem.

At major sites, such as forts, new notice-boards have been designed, so that people can share what has been discovered.

Events are organised at major sites close to roads, and the Ermine Street Guard's displays are popular. Soldiers march, throw javelins, demonstrate Roman fire-power against targets, and have their tents and other equipment on display. On a more gentle, domestic level, crafts and cooking are sometimes demonstrated, but posters concentrate on the warlike part of the story. Children, on school parties, dress up and 'become Romans' for their visit in cardboard armour, reinforcing this emphasis.

So, public access and the presentation of Roman life are not always a success, and the strategy will have to be constantly examined and revised. How we view history is important, and we must select carefully.

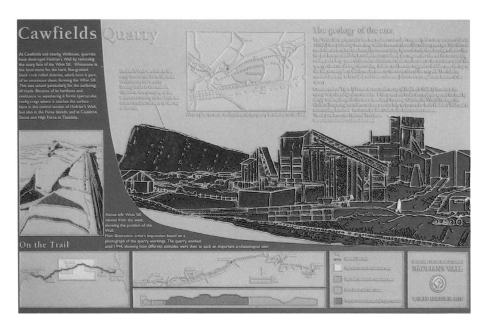

131. The presentation of sites to the public is a major concern today, as the Wall is such an important attraction. At Cawfields, it is good to see a board that tells the story of whinstone quarrying there.

132. At Vindolanda, a very important construction on a site previously archaeologically investigated was the building of a replica stone wall, stone turrets, wooden tower, and turf wall. Not only does this give a sense of scale and achievement, but it also gave an insight into how much work and planning was needed even for this small section.

133. Replica wooden tower.

134. Replica turret and initial turf wall.

135. South Shields: although the Fort is not covered in this book, the replica gateway there gives another important sense of scale.

136. Museums on site are particularly important. This one at Vindolanda is not only an
attractive building in a lovely setting, but also a means of sharing with its essential visitors
the ever-changing story of what is revealed each year. It is also an important refuge when
it rains and a place of sustenance – an essential consideration for families.

137. A model of a fort at Chesters

138. Birdoswald: a painting of what the site might have looked like after the Roman army left, based on its excavation.

139. The Ermine Street Guard appears frequently to demonstrate Roman equipment and tactics.

140. The Guard shares its tactics with the public.

141. Vindolanda provides the friendliest and most informative contact with visitors, as we see here, where Justin is one of the many archaeologists who gives children 'hands-on' experience of real objects found there, and makes them welcome.

FINALE

To complete this selection of images, I asked Lindsay Allason-Jones, who specialises, among other things, in Roman artefacts, and Robin Birley, who heads the Vindolanda Research Committee, to choose objects that are particularly significant to them, out of the hundreds that they have investigated. I have added images of a recent discovery that I witnessed recently at Vindolanda.

142. Lindsay's choice: Tombstone of Regina, a British woman who was the freedwoman and wife of Barates, a Palmyrene from Syria. The Military Zone had people from all over the Empire amongst its population. Regina died aged 30 at South Shields. (Newcastle University).

143. Lindsay's choice: The Aemilia finger ring from Corbridge, thought to be the earliest Christian artefact in Roman Britain. When Christianity was introduced into Britain, it was regarded as just another Eastern mystery cult, before it became the state religion of the fourth century. (Newcastle University).

144. Lindsay's choice: A building inscription set up by the centuries of Liburnius Fronto and Tarentius Magnus, of the Fourth Cohort of the Twentieth Legion Valeria Victrix. Found at Newburn. Legionary standards flank the inscription, which also shows the Imperial Eagle. (Newcastle University).

145. Lindsay's choice: The Rudge Cup. Found in Wiltshire in 1725, it shows the Wall and names of some of the forts in the Western Sector. It was probably intended as a souvenir of Hadrian's Wall, bought by a soldier who served there.

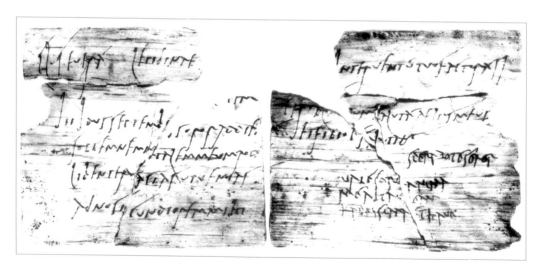

146. Robin Birley's choice: The birthday party invitation from Claudia Severa to Sulpicia Lepidena.

147. Robin's choice: A rare jet betrothal medallion from the Severan period.

148. Robin's choice: A rare find of a leather chamfron, ceremonial headpiece for a horse. Only one other good example exists, at Newstead.

149. Robin's choice: Glass decorated with a scene depicting gladiators.

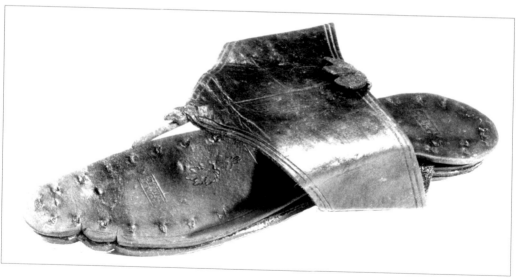

150. Robin's choice: Sulpicia Lepidina's dainty slipper, with the maker's stamp, from the third timber Fort.

151. The altar found in 2009 in the north-west quadrant inside the fort wall at Vindolanda illustrates how important the programme of excavation is there to our understanding of the life and beliefs of people living there.

152. Jupiter Dolichenus is depicted with an axe in one hand, and arrows in the other. His cult emerged in Britain at the time of Emperor Severus in the third century.

153. The inscription reads: To Jupiter Best and Greatest of Doliche Sulpicius Pudens prefect of the Fourth Cohort of Gauls fulfilled his vows gladly and deservedly.

154. Vindolanda in April 2010: the discovery of another round-house foundation in the north-west quadrant of the last stone fort.

BIBLIOGRAPHY

This is a general selection, but also contains other bibliographies for readers who want to pursue topics in depth, particularly listed in Breeze and Dobson (below)

Allason-Jones, L. 1989 *Women in Roman Britain* (London)

Bidwell, P. and Hodgson, N. 2009. The Roman Army in Northern England (The Arbeia Society, South Shields)

Bidwell, P. (ed). 2008. *Understanding Hadrian's Wall* (Arbeia Society, South Shields)

Birley, A. 2002. *Garrison life at Vindolanda* (Tempus)

Birley, R. 2009. *Vindolanda* (Amberley)

Breeze, D. and Dobson, B. 2000. *Hadrian's Wall* Fourth Edition. (Penguin)

Breeze, D. 2006. *J. Collingwood Bruce's Handbook to the Roman Wall* (Newcastle)

Hill, P. 2006. *The Construction of Hadrian's Wall* (Tempus)

Crowe, J. *Housesteads* (London)

Hodgson, N. 2009. Hadrian's Wall 1999-2009: A summary of excavation and research. (Ian Caruana, Carlisle)

Johnson, S. 1989. *Hadrian's Wall* (English Heritage)

Symands, M. and Mason, M. 2009. *Frontiers of Knowledge: a research framework for Hadrian's Wall* (Durham County Council)

Rushworth, A. 2009. *Housesteads.* English Heritage

Willmott, T. (ed). 2009. *Hadrian's Wall: archaeological research by English Heritage Co. 1976-2000* (English Heritage)

INDEX

The page number is given first followed by the Section A or B image reference number.

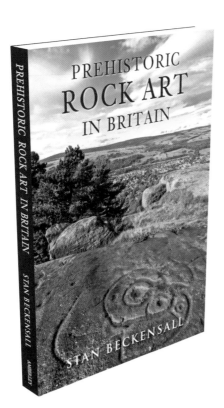